MARCH OF THE PENGUINS

MARCH OF THE PENGUINS

FROM THE FILM BY **LUC JACQUET**
NARRATION WRITTEN BY **JORDAN ROBERTS**
PHOTOGRAPHY BY **JÉRÔME MAISON**

NATIONAL GEOGRAPHIC
WASHINGTON, D.C.

Published by arrangement with Bonne Pioche/APC and Warner Bros. Entertainment Inc.

The text is set in Futura by Adobe.

Photographs copyright © 2004 Jérôme Maison/Bonne Pioche,
except as follows: p. 11,
copyright © Bill Curtsinger/National Geographic Society;
pp. 18-19, p. 22 bottom, p. 31 top, copyright © Frank Todd/www.arcticphoto.co.uk; pp. 20-21, copyright © Bill Curtsinger;p. 22 top and middle, copyright © 2004 Laurent Chalet/Bonne Pioche; p. 30, copyright © Doug Allen/www.naturepl.com.

Library of Congress Cataloging-in-Publication Information is available
from the Library of Congress upon request.

ISBN 0-7922-6183-6 (paperback)
ISBN 0-7922-6190-9 (library)

WARNER INDEPENDENT PICTURES and NATIONAL GEOGRAPHIC FEATURE FILMS PRESENT a BONNE PIOCHE PRODUCTION IN ASSOCIATION WITH WILD BUNCH "MARCH OF THE PENGUINS" AS TOLD BY MORGAN FREEMAN MUSIC BY ALEX WURMAN EDITOR SABINE EMILIANI CINEMATOGRAPHY LAURENT CHALET JERÔME MAISON EXECUTIVE PRODUCER ILANN GIRARD PRODUCED BY YVES DARONDEAU CHRISTOPHE LIOUD EMMANUEL PRIOU BASED UPON THE STORY BY LUC JACQUET BASED UPON THE SCREENPLAY BY LUC JACQUET & MICHEL FESSLER NARRATION WRITTEN BY JORDAN ROBERTS DIRECTED BY LUC JACQUET WITH THE PARTICIPATION OF BUENA VISTA INTERNATIONAL FILM PRODUCTION (FRANCE) AND CANAL+ A CO-PRODUCTION WITH APC IN ASSOCIATION WITH THE FRENCH POLAR INSTITUTE (IPEV)

BONNE PIOCHE   NATIONAL GEOGRAPHIC Feature Films   G GENERAL AUDIENCES All Ages Admitted   WARNER INDEPENDENT PICTURES

www.marchofthepenguins.com

One of the world's largest nonprofit scientific and educational organizations,
the National Geographic Society was founded in 1888 "for the increase and diffusion of
geographic knowledge." Fulfilling this mission, the Society educates and inspires millions every day
through its magazines, books, television programs, videos, maps and atlases, research grants,
the National Geographic Bee, teacher workshops, and innovative classroom materials.
The Society is supported through membership dues, charitable gifts,
and income from the sale of its educational products.
This support is vital to National Geographic's mission to increase global understanding
and promote conservation of our planet through exploration, research, and education.

For more information, please call
1-800-NGS-LINE (647-5463) or write to the following address:

NATIONAL GEOGRAPHIC SOCIETY

1145 17th Street N.W.
Washington, D.C. 20036-4688 U.S.A.
Visit the Society's Web site: www.nationalgeographic.com

PRINTED IN U.S.A.

This is Antarctica, the harshest place in the world to live. The average temperature is 40 degrees below zero, and that's in the summertime.

Very few animals call Antarctica home. That's good news for emperor penguins. When they come out on land, they have the place almost all to themselves.

It is March. Here in the southern hemisphere, summer is over, and winter is about to begin. The penguins have been feeding in the ocean for three months.

Now their bellies are full, so they bound out of the sea to go …

... on a very long walk.

They must walk day and night, sometimes for more than a week. They are on their way to their nesting ground 100 miles away.

When they get tired of walking, they give their feet a rest and slide on their bellies instead.

Finally the penguins arrive at the nesting ground. This is where every one of them was born. Their parents were born here, too. So were their grandparents.

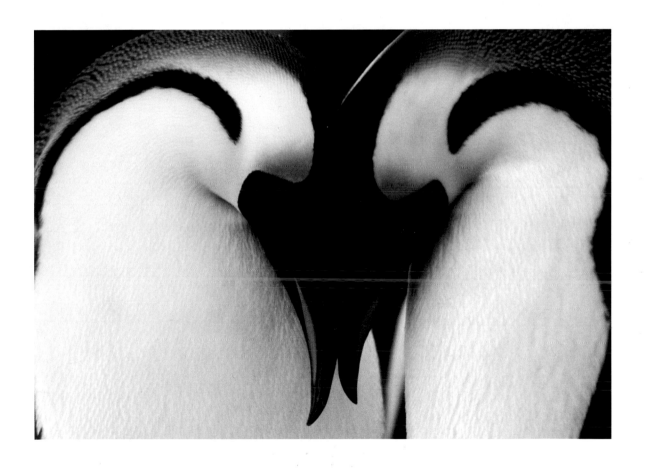

Here they will find their mates and start their families.

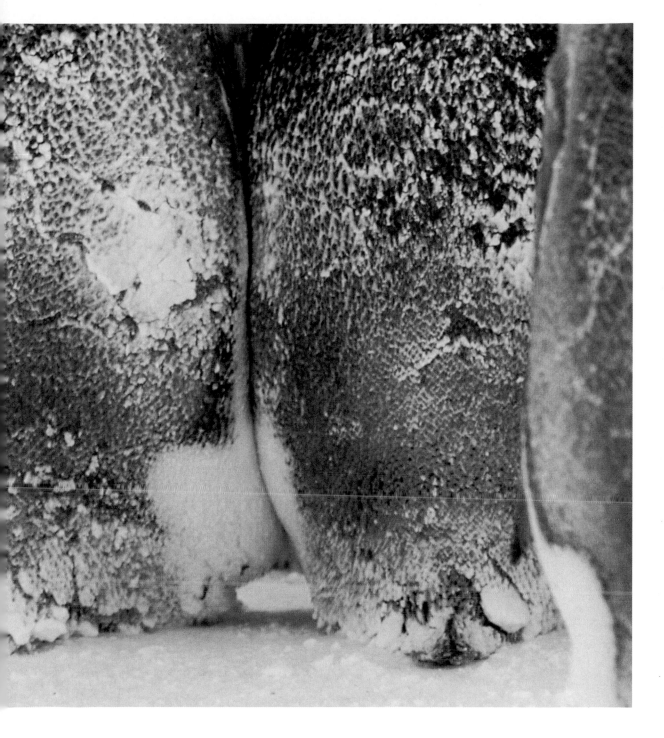

Soon winter descends, with high winds and freezing temperatures. The sun has set and will not rise until spring. The penguins huddle together against the cold, waiting.

One day in early June, in the very middle of winter, the females start laying their eggs.

As soon as the eggs are laid, the mothers must return to the sea to eat. But before they leave, each mother carefully passes her egg to its father. It's a very delicate process.

The father makes a nest for the egg on his feet, keeping it safe and warm beneath a flap of skin on his belly.

While the fathers care for the eggs, the exhausted mothers march. The moon and stars light their way.

Miles of new ice have formed along the shore, so they must walk even farther this time. When the mothers finally get to the sea, they are eager to take the plunge.

Water is the penguins' true home. They can hold their breath for over 15 minutes and dive to a depth of over 1,700 feet to feed on fish, krill, and squid.

Finally, winter begins its slow retreat.

Light returns to the South Pole.

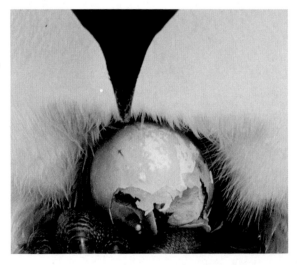

It is time for the eggs to hatch.

This newly hatched chick is hungry, but his mother hasn't arrived to feed him yet. The father penguin coughs up a milky liquid. Even though he hasn't eaten in over 100 days, he has kept this tiny meal in a small crease in his throat, just for his baby.

Then the mothers return full of food for themselves and their babies. The hungry fathers give the babies to their mothers and set off for the sea.

Like the sunlight, the chicks grow stronger every day. First they perch on their mothers' feet.

Then it is time to take their first steps.

For the next several months, as the chicks explore and grow, the parents take turns traveling back and forth to the sea for food. The chicks spend more time together.

But that doesn't mean they forget their parents.

It is now December, the middle of summer, and the chicks are almost grown. They are ready to leave the place where they were born. Although they have never even touched the ocean, they somehow know that it is where they are supposed to go. So, one day they take the plunge and go home for the very first time.

For four years, the chicks will live at sea. But as the warm days begin to cool at the end of their fifth year, they will know that their time has come.

They will bound out of the water.

They will march.

And they will spend the winter huddled together …

... bringing new life to Antarctica.